Create a Lifetime of Special Moments with Your Teen

Weekly Activities & Conversation Openers to Keep You Connecting

ANIKA VASSELL

GW00504096

Create a Life-Time of Special Moments with Your Teen:
Weekly Activities & Conversation Openers
to Keep You Connecting

Published by Starburst Educational Support Services

Join our Facebook group of supportive parents of teens & pre-teens- for professional advice, tips & a bit of fun!

Simply search & send your request to join:

'The Parents of Teenagers Village Community'

...because it still takes a village to raise a child

See you there!

DEDICATION

My girls – hold onto the words of wisdom spoken by your loved ones and by those who truly care about your future success and happiness.

Keep their words close to your hearts & use them to guide your decisions as you travel down your life chosen pathways.

ACKNOWLEDGEMENTS

A warm thank you to the children & young people whom I have met and worked with throughout my life.

I feel truly blessed to have been part of yours.

With a mixture of laughter, a little one-to-one time and a sprinkle of fun; these weekly activities and conversation openers will strengthen your bond during the 'tricky' adolescent years.

Why This Book?

This book has been filled with littlle gems of doable activities and converstaion openers that will keep you connecting with your teen or pre-teenaged child.

In this world of speed and technolgy, the time we spend together in our family units is getting less & less and unfortunately this leads to our children growing up and away from us.

This book will keep you sharing positive experiences and will help you to stay part of who your child is growing to be.

Together, your laughter; honesty and sharing; with a healthy sprinkle of silliness, will bring balance to an often 'tricky' and tense period which occurs in the lives of most families with adolescent aged children.
The weekly suggestions are there for you to adapt and use at you will.

You may experience some early resistence from your teen against some of the activities that you suggest - but persevere and don't give up too easily. More often than not, they will grow to love and will look forward to spending this positive time together - no matter how high they manage to roll their eyes at you!

Follow this concise guide and I promise that you will go on to create moments that will be loved and cherished by you both for years to come.

Enjoy!

"SOMETIMES IT'S JUST GOOD
TO STOP, SIT DOWN AND TAKE
JOY IN SEEING HOW FAR
WE'VE COME"

~ Anika Vassell ~

Special Moment - Week No.1

REFLECTION

It's amazing how easily we can get laser focused on the negatives. We are often the harshest critics of ourselves and our most loved ones.

Today, sit down with your teen and on a clean sheet of notepaper, make a list of all of the things that they have achieved over the past year.

Write down all of their personal and academic achievements as well as positive contributions they have made within the family home.

In addition write down anything where they have shown progression and positive moves forward towards bettering themselves and/or for the better of others. This could be a simple act of kindness such as being a listening ear for a friend.

When you've finished – pop it in an envelope and give it to them to take away.

"WE TEND TO BECOME LIKE THOSE WHOM WE ADMIRE"

~Thomas S. Monson ~

Special Moment - Week No.2

HELD IN HIGH ESTEEM

Find out who your child holds admiration for.

There may be different people in different settings and they may be admired for very different reasons.

Find out exactly what it is about this person that your child admires? Are they kind, ambitious or fun?

Consider what are the positive qualities that this person has that your child could also possess.

Now, nobody is perfect and you might not think much of their 'idol' but generally - even within the most unsavory of characters - there will be some good traits – somewhere.

It's okay to give the flaws you may spot just a brief mention, but focus more on that individual's positives.

"WHEN WE GIVE WE ARE ALWAYS REWARDED WITH SO MUCH MORE"

~ Anika Vassell ~

Special Moment - Week No.4

VOLUNTEERING

Volunteering doesn't have to be on a grand scale. It doesn't even have to be committing time on a regular basis. Many events will be held in and around your community that will be 'one-offs'.

Volunteering could be simple acts of kindness, such as helping a neighbour or elderly family member with a little garden maintenance or painting a gate for instance. Whatever it is – the act of giving is a powerful one.

Find out what's happening in your community and sign both yourself and your teen up.

You may have to really coax them with this one but the psychology behind helping others shows that the emotional rewards for the giver equals, if not outweighs those of the receiver.

If helping others also means you will work side-by-side whilst bonding with your teen - then this activity has to get a big thumbs-up!

"FOOD IS THE WAY TO EVERYONE'S HEART"

~ Anika Vassell ~

Special Moment - Week No.5

TIME TO COOK UP SOMETHING GOOD

In this instance 'good' won't necessarily coincide with your ideas of 'good' – this is totally about your teen.

Find out what their favourite meal would consist of and just go with the flow of their weird and wonderful ideas.

Get right into the details – from the music playing in the background, to the lighting that would accompany the meal…
… and don't forget the desert!

This could become a regular feature - once a week or, if your child has made particularly expensive choices (or unhealthy ones) - once a month.

It will be just as rewarding for you as the parent to prepare their chosen meal and watch them enjoying the fruits of your labour!

"SILENCE CAN CREATE GOLDEN MOMENTS"

~ Anika Vassell ~

Special Moment - Week No.6

SSSH!

Make a herbal tea for you both, switch everything off and during a moment of stillness, sit down and just enjoy each other's company.

Without the buzz of gadgets and phones you'll create a space for both of you to just stop and be with your thoughts.

Quite time is wonderfully therapeutic.
It is also a time that any underlying worries have the opportunity to bubble to the surface.

It's a time where you can generate some very meaningful conversations and moments with your teen.

If a conversation surfaces - just go with the flow and listen out for what is on their mind.

If your teen enters the room with something on their mind then mute or pause the tv. They will appreciate you giving them your full attention.

It doesn't have to be an epic event either - ten minutes will beat zero minutes hands down.

"MUSIC, AT ITS ESSENCE, IS WHAT GIVES US MEMORIES. THE LONGER A SONG HAS EXISTED IN OUR LIVES, THE MORE MEMORIES WE HAVE OF IT"

~ Stevie Wonder ~

Special Moment - Week No.7

SONG PERSONALITIES

Together, think of songs that represent members of your family.

Now, your aim is not to offend others so if the songs are funny or are ironic - ensure they are light-hearted as once you label a person with a particular song, it will stick!

Next, think of positive songs for one another.

What is it about the song that reminds you of them?

What message is in the song lyrics do you want your teen to hold on to?

Music is a powerful trigger for our memories and emotions. Any time that particular song is heard in the future, both you and your teen will think of one another and you will remember the time when you created that moment together.

Ahh!

"ENTHUSIASM IS EXCITEMENT WITH INSPIRATION, MOTIVATION, AND A PINCH OF CREATIVITY"

~ **Bo Bennett** ~

Special Moment – Week No.8

SHARE THE ENTHUSIASM

You: "How was school?" **Your Teen:** "Fine"
You: Did you learn anything new or exciting?
Your Teen: No, not really **You:** Oh.
End of conversation!

Sound familiar?

In an establishment of learning, you can be very much
assured that every day your child would have the
opportunity to discover something that would have
totally blown them away.

Understanding new concepts and applying them to the
real world is amazing!

They will have learnt about things that they didn't even
know that they didn't know.

They could have been involved in a huge and heated
class debate. It could have been an experiment that
they conducted in the science lab or a new skill that
they mastered on the sports field.

Maybe one of their friends said or did something so
'random' that it sent them into a fit of giggles.

Ask your teen to share and then show your interest and
enthusiasm when they do. Your energy will be catching!

"THERE ARE JUST SO MANY STORIES THAT ARE BURIED ON FAMILY TREES"

~ Henry Louis Gates ~

Special Moment – Week No.9

STORIES FROM THE FAMILY TREE

Drawing a tree to represent your family's history is a beautiful way to spend time together.

There is something that runs deep within, and centres us when we create visual representations and give new consideration of our family connections.

Your teen will find something satisfying in understanding how all of the pieces fit together to make them who they are.

Each branch has a story to tell.

See which stories you can share that will help your teen to develop connections with the relatives who are around them now and those who have gone before.

You can get really creative with this one.

If you have photos of family members then even better - add them to the tree.
Maybe, together, you could craft one as a gift for another family member.

Do this and your teen will develop a deeper sense of belonging and a respect for their history, connecting their past, present and their future.

"TRUE ENJOYMENT COMES FROM
ACTIVITY OF THE MIND AND
EXERCISE OF THE BODY; THE
TWO ARE EVER UNITED"

~ Wilhelm von Humboldt ~

Special Moment - Week No.10

KEEP THE TICKER TICKING

Instilling a positive attitude towards a healthy lifestyle in your teen is beneficial and a way of life that should always be encouraged.

Not everybody likes exercise but everyone can benefit from the results.

The great thing is that there are many different ways that you can enjoy an active lifestyle with your teen.

A bike ride, a run or a simple walk on a regular basis will be great for you and great for them.

Just imagine the amount of opportunities that will be created to talk to each other.

This is what is generally known at Starburst-ESS Headquarters as a

Win! Win!

"WE CAN LIVE WITHOUT RELIGION AND MEDITATION, BUT WE CANNOT SURVIVE WITHOUT HUMAN AFFECTION"

~ Dalai Lama ~

Special Moment – Week No.11

AFFECTION

The adolescent years are a time when hugs and cuddles can disappear altogether and both physical and emotional distance can develop between you.

There may be a number of reasons for this - the most overlooked one being that your child's body is developing and it may be that being physically close to you at this time feels uncomfortable or a little awkward.

Whilst respecting their personal space, don't give up on them. If your child seems to be giving you the cold shoulder - just hold onto the fact that it is more likely to be about them than you.

However, touch is an important part of your interaction and the continued bond that you maintain with your child. Think about how you can keep that nurturing physical connection without being too intrusive of their personal space.

Kind words; a touch on the arm for reassurance; a stroke on their face to show that you care.

There are still many things that you will be able to convey without going in for the full on bear hug.

If you can maintain these smaller gestures of affection through to the other side of adolescence, this will leave the door open for your teen to be close to you again.

"WORDS HAVE MEANING AND NAMES HAVE POWER."

~ Author Unknown ~

Special Moment – Week No.12

WHAT'S IN A NAME?

Well, so much actually!

The origins of names can be steeped in history &
culture. The same name may have different meanings
dependant on its origin.

If you are a creative person then you could make a
beautiful collage with your child's name at the centre;
showing the different influences that impacted on your
decision to settle on the name you chose for them.

Let them know what the alternative names were that
you concidered.

What kind of feelings did the names evoke when you
thought of them.

Whom does their name remind you of?

Who are the great people in your extended family or in
history with the same name as your teen?

Naming your child was a huge decision for you.

Let them know about the amount of love and
consideration that you put into that.

"WITHOUT REFLECTION, WE GO BLINDLY ON OUR WAY, CREATING MORE UNINTENDED CONSEQUENCES, AND FAILING TO ACHIEVE ANYTHING USEFUL."

~ Margaret J. Wheatley ~

Special Moment – week No.13

LIFE'S LESSONS

Personal reflection is an essential skill to nurture in your teen.

It will ensure that messages or signs from their environment are not ignored, left to drift or go by without notice.

Teach your teen to be reflective.

Questions they need to ask themselves are:

How does this impact on me now?
How will it impact on my future?
What role did I play?
Could I have done things differently?
What can I learn?

By asking these questions, your teen will understand how their own actions impact on events and how learning from past experiences can help shape their future choices.

Share some of your own personal reflections and let them know how this helped you to do things differently to generate different outcomes.

See if your teen has any personal reflections to share with you.

"A PICTURE IS A POEM WITHOUT WORDS"

~ Horace ~

Special Moment – Week No.14

PICTURE PERFECT

This is a simple and beautiful activity to share.

Frame a photo of yourself and give it to your teen.

If you can - make it a time from your youth; one of happiness; a time of personal growth or a special moment and share your story with them.

Allow your teen the space to imagine, view and get to know you as an individual, independent of your family title of 'Mom' or 'Dad'.

Let them know that you have had and still do experience great emotions, joys and exhilarations just as they do.

Let them know you in a different light.

"A LIFE SPENT MAKING
MISTAKES IS NOT ONLY MORE
HONOURABLE, BUT MORE
USEFUL THAN A LIFE SPENT
DOING NOTHING"

~ **George Bernard Shaw** ~

Special Moment – Week No.15

MISTAKES DO HAPPEN!

What does your teen think about the mistakes that they have made?

Have they been totally devastated and discouraged by the consequences of their actions or have they taken them as lessons to be learned in life?

The only mistake your child can make is in not learning from them.

Find out what lessons they have learnt this week.

"MY PARENTS ARE MY BACKBONE. STILL ARE. THEY'RE THE ONLY GROUP THAT WILL SUPPORT YOU IF YOU SCORE ZERO OR YOU SCORE FORTY"

~ Kobe Bryant ~

Special Moment – Week No.16

SUPPORT FROM THE SIDE-LINES

With time playing a major factor in most family's lives - it can get harder and harder to support them in their interests and activities – however, even just showing up can be paramount!

Without your presence, their victories will feel empty and defeats will be just that bit harder to take.

Do they play football? Are they in a band or a school play? Figure out how you can best demonstrate your support for them and go out of your way, every once in a while to be there.

You might not make it weekly but the effort to be there at crucial events (even when they tell you 'it's no big deal') is so important.

After the dust has settled - your presence will give their experience meaning and will avoid your absence or lack of support being the main feature of their memory.

"PHOTOGRAPH: A PICTURE PAINTED BY THE SUN WITHOUT INSTRUCTION IN ART"

~ Ambrose Bierce ~

Special Moment – Week No.17

WORTH A THOUSAND WORDS

Ask your teen to share a picture of themselves. Ask them to find one that captured a moment of happiness.

It might be a picture of them with their friends or family members; it might be one of them on holiday or participating in an activity.

Talk about the time and what made the moment so special.

With most photos spending their life-time filed on the computer, take this one and print it off.

Frame it and put it in your room or display it in a prominent position within your home.

You and your teen can now take pleasure in the memory every time you see it.

EVERY PERSON HAS A LONGING
TO BE SIGNIFICANT; TO MAKE A
CONTRIBUTION; TO BE A PART
OF SOMETHING NOBLE AND
PURPOSEFUL.

~ John C. Maxwell ~

Special Moment – Week No.17

WHAT DO YOU THINK?

Seeking your child's opinion on the decisions that will impact on them is an important part of keeping the connection between you.

Seeking their opinion is what matters as it shows a clear demonstration of your respect for them.

Consult with your teen whenever you can and whenever it is appropriate to do so.

Ask their opinion and be respectful towards the contribution that they make.

Just remind them that a decision will have to be made that will take everyone's views into consideration.

It may not go 'their way' but you will see how you can incorporate their ideas as you best can.

"DANCING IS LIKE DREAMING WITH YOUR FEET! "

~ Constanze ~

Special Moment - Week No.18

BOOGIE IN A BOX!

On slips of paper, write down the names of your favourite songs. Fold them up and put them in a box.

On a morning – when you have a little time – take turns to pick one of the slips out and surprise yourselves with the song that you have chosen.

Use the internet to find the song, turn the volume up and sing and dance away!

There is no better way to start your morning than with a little boogie before breakfast!

"I LOVE SHARING MY STORY. IT'S ENDLESSLY HEALING."

~ Ben Vereen ~

Special Moment - Week No.19

JOBS WORTH

Share some of your stories about the jobs that you have held or the career paths you have chosen during your own teen years or early twenties.

Did you meet anybody interesting who influenced the paths you chose?

What was your boss like?

What about your work colleagues?

Did you have any awkward customers?

Did you wriggle out of an awkward situation?

Share a funny moment.

"CHOOSE A CAREER YOU LOVE, GIVE IT THE BEST THERE IS IN YOU, SEIZE YOUR OPPORTUNITIES, AND BE A MEMBER OF THE TEAM"

~ Benjamin Franklin Fairless ~

Special Moment - Week No.20

CAREER CHOICES

Find out about the future careers your teen can picture themselves in.

Why have they thought of this one?

What would it be like?

What experiences would they hope to have?

What skills are required in a job such as that?

What skills would they need to develop in order to be successful in the role?

Of those skills, which ones do they already have?

If there is anyone that either of you know in that field – could they speak to them about what they do?

Have a browse of the internet together and research the possibilities.

"JUST AS IN LIFE; A TRULY
WONDERFUL & ADVENTUROUS
SEA JOURNEY IS NEVER
ACHIEVED THROUGH
PLAIN SAILING"

~ Anika Vassell ~

Special Moment - Week No.21

TIME FOR MORE SHARING

Often children & young people believe that life should come easier than it actually does.

It's okay for the illusion to be shattered if you can also show how, every day, people face and overcome hardships.

Often we give examples of great leaders outside of the family but today try something a little closer to home.

Make reference to the people whom they know; whom they can actually relate to and identify with.

Share some of the struggles that you have faced and have overcome.

Give examples of your own perseverance and dedication.

We all have a story to tell so today, share it with your teen.

"REMEMBER THAT THE HAPPIEST PEOPLE ARE NOT THOSE GETTING MORE, BUT THOSE GIVING MORE"

~ H. Jackson Brown, Jr. ~

Special Moment - Week No.22

A SPECIAL MOMENT FOR YOU.

As mentioned earlier on - there is no greater reward
than to give.

So, why not give your teen the opportunity
to create a special moment for you?

Chose a day, synchronise your diaries, and let them
know the following…

The songs you would like to hear playing

The meal that you would most enjoy them making for
you.

What film you would most like to watch with them
afterwards.

Anything you like – ask and you should receive.

They'll love creating this special moment for you as
much as you will enjoy receiving it.

"ALWAYS SEEK OUT THE SEED OF TRIUMPH IN EVERY ADVERSITY"

~ Og Mandino ~

Special Moment - Week No.23

FLIP IT

The power or the mind is awesome - we are still a long way off from knowing the extent of its full capabilities.

With the right mindset, your teen can flip many of the struggles and obstacles that they face right over.

What struggles has your teen faced and overcome recently?

Do they recognise the triumphs that they have made at school, at home or in their out-of-school activities?

Help them to identify when facing past challenges, they have shown the characteristics of: Perseverance; Dedication; Hope & Determination.

How did it feel when they overcame adversity?

What lessons did they take away?

If faced with a similar situation what would they do differently?

How will they think differently in the future?

"WE'RE A WORK IN PROGRESS. DO NOT BE ASHAMED OR AFRAID TO ASK FOR HELP. THAT'S WHAT I DID. I ASKED FOR HELP"

~ Carnie Wilson ~

Special Moment - Week No.24

IT REALLY IS OKAY!

Fact: Your teen won't always turn to you for help!

In most cases this is not such a bad thing as it means that your teen is being resourceful and working things out for themselves.

However, you don't want them to lock things up inside & struggle on without seeking support if the support is needed.

Whilst it is often perceived as a weakness; seeking help and support from others is an important life skill.

Help them to build their own wall of personal support around them.

Together, discuss and make a list of people whom they can turn to if they are ever struggling in areas such as:

relationships
personal concerns
school worries

Your teen needs to know that it is more than okay to ask for help.

Success is rarely achieved alone!

"A WONDERFUL THING ABOUT TRUE
LAUGHTER IS THAT IT JUST DESTROYS ANY
KIND OF SYSTEM OF DIVIDING PEOPLE."

~ John Cleese ~

Special Moment - Week No.25

FAMILY FUN & LAUGHTER

Classic board games, card games, or charades are great activities for spending quality time together.

Some of these games can go on for hours and in the spirit of fun - a bit of a competitive edge is great

Set a time in your diary - it could be on a monthly basis – but just commit.

Your teen could invite friends over, dependent on how willing you are for your gathering to grow - it could be a real social occasion with food, drinks; and the whole shebang!

"IT DOESN'T TAKE MONEY TO TURN OFF THE TELEVISION AND CULTIVATE REAL BONDING TIME."

~ Marianne Williamson ~

Special Moment - Week No.26

JUST GET THE JOB DONE!

This week, synchronise your diaries and book in a time to tackle a big job together. It might be:

gardening
clearing a room
decorating
decluttering
clearing out the shed

If it's a job that you have been putting off for a while – then this is ideal.

Working together will make the task so much easier and is also a great opportunity for a bit of bonding time.

This week, tick an item off, from your to-do-list and get connecting with your teen.

Another Win! Win!

Just how we like them!

"DO NOT DWELL IN THE PAST,
DO NOT DREAM OF THE FUTURE,
CONCENTRATE THE MIND ON
THE PRESENT MOMENT."

~ Buddha ~

Special Moment - Week No.27

MINDFUL MOMENTS

We spend a lot of time thinking of the past and we spend a lot of time thinking about the future but we don't spend enough time thinking of the present moment.

Encourage your child to take notice and enjoy what is happening here, right now! Show them how to use their five senses in order to concentrate their thoughts.

What can they see? The contrasting colours? The light and the shade?

What can they hear? – The birds? The sound of their own breathing?

What can they smell in their environment? The summer air or a smell that indicates rain is on its way?

What can they taste? Are there explosions of flavours? Can they feel the crunch and sweetness of an apple?

What can they feel? How does the rug feel beneath their feet? How does it feel to hold a hand?

We often miss the greatness of right now.

SELF-LOVE IS THE SOURCE OF ALL OUR OTHER LOVES.

~ Pierre Corneille ~

Special Moment - Week No 28

ME TIME

Think of the things that your teen can do to spend a
little extra time just for themselves.

It might be a long bath with special bath salts
or some time reading a self-development book or it
may be watching a comedy or their favourite movie.

Let the agenda be nothing but to fulfil what they want
for themselves, not for you, not to impress their
friends, not for family – just for them.

Allow them that space & ask how they feel afterwards.

"I CAN'T IMAGINE WANTING TO BE FAMOUS JUST FOR THE SAKE OF BEING FAMOUS. I THINK FAME SHOULD COME ALONG WITH SUCCESS, TALENT."

~ Kat Dennings ~

Special Moment - Week No.29

FAME & FORTUNE

In this rag to riches world of quick fame which is then televised for the masses, many children strive to be 'famous' and go to extraordinary lengths to get there.

Here's your chance to find out if your child wants to be famous and if so, why?

What would they want to be known for?

What would they do with the fame that they acquired?

What do they feel fame would bring?

Do they know of any consequences to living a life in the public eye?

What about the responsibilities?

Can a person be successful without being rich & famous?

Help your son or daughter to see the reality behind the glitz and glamour.

"FOR GOOD IDEAS AND TRUE INNOVATION, YOU NEED HUMAN INTERACTION, CONFLICT, ARGUMENT, DEBATE."

~ Margaret Heffernan ~

Special Moment - Week No.30

WHAT'S YOUR POINT?

News events can be used to trigger in-depth conversation with your teen.

Don't miss the opportunity to get to know & understand your teen a little better.

Show respect for their views on current affairs.

There are often different perspectives and different sides to the same argument and they may not see things in the same way as you do.

Show that you understand them even if you may not agree with them.

Fostering a strong opinion on topics, whilst still being able to empathise with others is a healthy characteristic.

Debate with your teen - it's a fantastic skill to nurture in them.

"THE MORE YOU PRAISE AND CELEBRATE YOUR LIFE, THE MORE THERE IS IN LIFE TO CELEBRATE."

~ Oprah Winfrey ~

Special Moment - Week No. 31

RECOGNITION

Think of three special things that your teen has done this month, this week or today.

Have they made you smile?

When?

Why?

Did you see them triumph over an obstacle?

Did they show an act of kindness or caring?

There is no better person to share your thoughts with. Let them know about all of the good that you see in them!

"WE CANNOT TEACH PEOPLE ANYTHING; WE CAN ONLY HELP THEM DISCOVER IT WITHIN THEMSELVES."

~ Galileo Galilei ~

Special Moment - Week No.32

KNOCK! KNOCK!

If your teen is stuck with a dilemma, sometimes they just won't let you in!

However, forcing the issue can have the effect of pushing them deeper into their solitude.

If you can see that they are worried, feeling low or unsure of what to do with themselves – then simply let them know that you are there if they need you and give them their space for now.

You can then approach them later, during a period of calm and ask:

"If this happens again, what would you like me to do next time?

Is there anything that can do now, that would help you out?

Is there anybody else whom you could speak to?

Weather they chose to take you up on their offer of support or not – the one thing they will not be able to question is your support for them.

"KEEP ALL SPECIAL THOUGHTS
AND MEMORIES FOR LIFETIMES
TO COME. SHARE THESE
KEEPSAKES WITH OTHERS TO
INSPIRE HOPE AND BUILD FROM
THE PAST, WHICH CAN BRIDGE
TO THE FUTURE."

~ Mattie Stepanek ~

Special Moment - Week No 33

SHARE IN THEIR MOMENTS

What are the three special things that have happened to them this week?

Have they spent time in somebody's company that uplifted them?

Has someone made them smile?

Has there been an act of kindness by a sibling, a friend, or a teacher?

Did anything happen which really made them laugh this week?

Share in the special moments that they have experienced.

Listen to their stories.

"I LOVE TO HAVE A BATH WITH
BEAUTIFUL, RELAXING MUSIC ON
AND HAVE NO RUSH TO DO
ANYTHING. IT'S A WONDERFUL
INDULGENCE, AND IT HELPS ME
TO CALM DOWN AND STOP MY
MIND RUNNING OVERTIME."

~ Kylie Minogue ~

Special Moment - Week 34

ORGANISE A PAMPER DAY

This one may involve a little expense and it is certainly not restricted to mothers and daughters only!

a massage
a facial
nails done
a spa day
the hairdressers

There are some lovely discounted offers that you can find on the internet.

If ever you're a bit flush then take yourselves out and get yourselves pampered together!

"YOU HAVE TO DREAM BEFORE YOUR DREAMS CAN COME TRUE."

~ A. P. J. Abdul Kalam ~

Special Moment - Week No.35

DREAMER

When we dream of something it is often of a seemingly impossible goal.

Is there something that your child dreams of doing?

Has their dream ever been done before? If it has then this immediately turns their dream into something that is possible.

What could they do to make that dream come true?

What can they do to get as near to that dream as they can?

Is it something that you could help them with?

Can it be broken down into small steps at a time?

Map out the process and show them how, if they really want it, you can actually help them to plan and make their dreams come true.

"FRIENDSHIP IS THE SOURCE OF
THE GREATEST PLEASURES, AND
WITHOUT FRIENDS EVEN THE
MOST AGREEABLE PURSUITS
BECOME TEDIOUS."

~ Thomas Aquinas ~

Special Moment - Week No 36

WHO IS THIS PERSON?

It is important for you to know their friends.

Your teen's friends have so much influence over the decisions that they will make.

Your child may have turned to their friends to support them through things of magnitude and importance when you were not able to. Not because you didn't want to - but because it was something that your child chose not to confide in you.

Some of their friendships may last for your teen's lifetime – many years after you have passed away.

Regardless of your thoughts about your teen's friends – it is important to treat them well; with dignity and respect. Their friends may be more good for your child than you could ever imagine!

Why not take them out? A meal or to an activity?

Show your appreciation of them, they will appreciate you and in turn, your child will see and appreciate you.

"NEVER, EVER UNDERESTIMATE THE IMPORTANCE OF HAVING FUN."

~ Randy Pausch ~

Special Moment - Week No.37

EMBARRASSING PARENT ALERT!

Next time you go out shopping with your teen, why not take a break from the monotony, and have a dress up in something a little out of your comfort zone.

After making them promise not to post you up on any social media sites without your express permission - take a few selfies.

Vintage shops are especially good fun and - you never know - you might find a few classic items for you to add to your wardrobe collection too!

"SOME MEMORIES ARE UNFORGETTABLE, REMAINING EVER VIVID AND HEART-WARMING!"

~ Joseph B. Wirthlin ~

Special Moment - Week No.38

DOWN MEMORY LANE

Encourage your teen to identify and focus on the positive aspects that exist in their lives.

When things get tough, as they do, your child can use the good that is around them to put things back into perspective.

What is there most treasured memory from their family home?

at school?

on holiday?

with their friends?

an activity they participate in?

The great thing about memories is that they can be used at any time or place of your teen's choosing.

Share your treasured memories with them too.

"IT'S GREAT TO HAVE
SOMETHING TO DRESS UP FOR.
YOU KNOW, I SPENT THREE
YEARS IN SLACKS AT DRAMA
SCHOOL, SO NOW I LIKE
PUTTING A DRESS ON."

~ Lupita Nyong'o ~

Special Moment - Week No.39

DRESSED TO THE NINES

There is always a time during the year to get dressed up in your best!

Think of somewhere different and special whre you could take your son or daughter too.

Make it somewhere that would mean taking time for you both to get ready and prepared for the event.

Maybe the theatre; to a favourite restaurant, or to a charity ball.

Dressing up and going all out on the town with your teen is just lovely parent and teen connecting time.

"MORE THAN KISSES, LETTERS MINGLE SOULS."

~ John Donne ~

Special Moment - Week No. 40

SAY IT IN A LETTER
(or a little post-it note)

Every now and then leave little word treasures for your teen to find.

Write about something positive that you have seen happen to them.

Write about their kind acts that you have seen them carry out for you or for somebody else.

Write down how you feel about them.

Just little one-liners for them to find at unexpected times and in unexpected places.

"EDUCATION IS THE MOST POWERFUL
WEAPON WHICH YOU CAN USE TO CHANGE
THE WORLD."

~ Nelson Mandela ~

Special Moment - Week No.41

SCHOOL IS A HUGE PART OF THEIR LIVES

Education is important and some subjects or teachers in school will go on to positively impact upon your child for many years to come.

There is far more to school than grades.

So with that in mind, beyond the grades that they get –

What is the subject that your child is learning that they feel will be of the most benefit to them in the future and why?

Which subject do they feel will be of the least benefit? Is this true in your mind?

Do the subjects have real-life applications?

Having a discussion will generate more interest and expand their thinking beyond the exam grades which can easily become the sole focus of school.

"WHEN I LOOK OUT AT THE PEOPLE AND THEY LOOK AT ME AND THEY'RE SMILING, THEN I KNOW THAT I'M LOVED. THAT IS THE TIME WHEN I HAVE NO WORRIES, NO PROBLEMS."

~ Etta James ~

Special Moment - Week No 42

NO WORRIES

If your teen sometimes finds it difficult to approach you, then you can create a 'no worries' jar.

Simply put a jar in your room – somewhere away from other siblings and their prying eyes.

When your teen has a problem and they are not sure how to approach you, let them know that they can write about it and put their worry in the jar.

When you find their notes - schedule some quality time to address whatever it is that is bothering them.

Let them see that you are taking their thoughts and feelings seriously.

Don't forget to check the jar!

"NOTHING ENDURES BUT PERSONAL QUALITIES."

~ Walt Whitman ~

Special Moment - Week No. 43

BEST FRIENDS FOREVER

Friends can make you or break you.

Help your teen to identify the qualities that they believe a good friend should have.

Clarify with them the elements that should exist to create a positive friendship.

What is it that makes some relationships last and some fail?

Find out what qualities they will look out for, the next time they meet someone and a relationship begins to develop.

Help them to be clear on the type of people that they would like in their lives.

Ensure your teen is empowered to make active decisions in selecting who they want in their friendship and relationship circles.

"SOME MEMORIES ARE UNFORGETTABLE, REMAINING EVER VIVID AND HEART-WARMING!"

~ Joseph B. Wirthlin ~

Special Moment - Week No.44

ALL GROWN UP!

Sometimes teens can be so intent on growing up that they can forget just to have fun!

Help them to remember and rekindle those feelings of excitement from their childhood by involving them in something that they 'used-to' find fun.

It won't take them long to forget themselves.

Is there a favourite place or park that you used to visit together?

How about a game or activity that they used to enjoy?

Encourage that childlike element at every opportunity.

Never let them forget how to let go and how to have fun!

"IT'S OKAY TO GET IT WRONG.
THE LESSON COMES FROM THE
LEARNING AND DOING IT
DIFFERENTLY NEXT TIME."

~ Anika Vassell ~

Special Moment - Week No.45

OOPS!

Mistakes are a natural course of life.

We continually make mistakes and we continually correct ourselves.

Let your teen know that making mistakes is okay. It's when we don't learn from them that is the problem. Learning from mistakes is a key skill.

Today, with your teen, you can explore a little further into the 'mistakes' that they have made.

How does your child view their mistakes?

How do they feel after making a mistake?

Can they view mistakes as learning opportunities?

What measures can they put in place that will prevent them from making the same mistake again?

"THE GLORY OF GARDENING:
HANDS IN THE DIRT, HEAD IN
THE SUN, HEART WITH NATURE.
TO NURTURE A GARDEN IS TO
FEED NOT JUST ON THE BODY,
BUT THE SOUL."

~ Alfred Austin ~

Special Moment - Week No.46

MOTHER EARTH

Why not try planting a tree together?

Visit the garden centre and find a special tree – give it a meaning - a reason for choosing it and a reason for planting it in the spot which you chose to plant it.

It may represent the passing of a loved one or it may represent a triumph that your child has had.

Or, chose a tree simply because it bares your teen's favourite fruit.

Whatever your reason the tree will grow and stand grounded, as a symbol of strength for years to come.

"JUST AS WE DEVELOP OUR PHYSICAL MUSCLES THROUGH OVERCOMING OPPOSITION - SUCH AS LIFTING WEIGHTS - WE DEVELOP OUR CHARACTER MUSCLES BY OVERCOMING CHALLENGES AND ADVERSITY."

~ Stephen Covey

Special Moment - Week No.47

CHALLENGING TIMES

Challenge is necessary.

Your teen will be faced with challenges on a daily basis.

Life satisfaction is often measured through the amount of challenges faced and the amount of challenges that are overcome.

Regardless of wealth, race or culture - there will be many hurdles that your child will have to overcome in their lifetime.

Sometimes they come frequently sometimes there is more distance between them.

What strengths has your teen already demonstrated that will enable them to tackle any problem - no matter how big or small - that may come their way in the future?

See if they can identify their own strengths and highlight to them strengths which they may have overlooked

"I REALLY BELIEVE THAT EVERYONE HAS A
TALENT, ABILITY, OR SKILL THAT HE CAN
MINE TO SUPPORT HIMSELF AND TO
SUCCEED IN LIFE."

~ Dean Koontz ~

Special Moment - Week No.48

I NEVER SAW THAT IN ME!

There will be many things that your teen is very good at and there will be a few things that they are extremely talented at.

Sometimes it can be hard for your teen to distinguish one from the other.

Sometimes your teen will totally overlook their qualities and it will take another person to highlight a talent that they have never considered before.

Without showing one another – take a few minutes and each of you make a list of things that your teen is good at and a list of things that you can see they are highly talented at.

Compare your lists.

"IF YOU HAVE THE FEELING
THAT SOMETHING IS WRONG,
DON'T BE AFRAID TO SPEAK UP."

~ Fred Korematsu ~

Special Moment - Week No.49

HEAR MY VOICE

The best medicine and the quickest route to self-empowerment is to speak up and be heard.

Facing authority figures and challenging them in an appropriate way is a skill that can be taught and learnt.

When has your child wanted to challenge a teacher, but felt they couldn't?

When in the past have they wanted to challenge you?

What about a friend?

Support your teen and guide them with the words they could use and the approach that they could take which would result in challenging without triggering confrontation.

"WE DON'T NEED BIGGER CARS OR FANCIER CLOTHES. WE NEED SELF-RESPECT, IDENTITY, COMMUNITY, LOVE, VARIETY, BEAUTY, CHALLENGE AND A PURPOSE IN LIVING THAT IS GREATER THAN MATERIAL ACCUMULATION."

~ Donella Meadows ~

Special Moment - Week No.50

A BIGGER PURPOSE

A lot of emphasis is placed on making money and its link to success.

Whilst 'making money' is not a bad focus to have you can support your teen to see beyond that.

As humans, we are only truly fulfilled when we have a bigger, higher purpose that reaches beyond the materialistic.

What is your teen's bigger purpose?

What would they like to contribute to in order to make the world a better place to live in?

How will they do that?

Are there things that they can do now in order to contribute to that bigger purpose?

Set them on their way.

"YOU MAY HAVE MISSED THAT
PARTICULAR MOMENT BUT
THERE ARE LOTS OF FUTURE
MOMENTS TO COME. THEIR IS NO
HARM DONE IN JUST TRYING
AGAIN."

~ Anika Vassell ~

Special Moment - Week No.51

IS THERE SOMETHING I MISSED?

There may be times when you have totally missed an opportunity to address a particular issue with your teen.

It may be that you didn't pick up that their 'bad attitude' was related to another event in their lives that they were struggling to process.

Every now and then simply ask them…

"Has there been a time when I have missed that you were feeling upset?

Ask them to share what it was.

Explain to them that you wished that you had known about it.

Where they able to sort it out?

Is there anything that you can do to help now?

How will your teen help you to ensure that you don't miss a moment like that again?

"WHAT IS THE GOOD OF YOUR STARS AND TREES, YOUR SUNRISE AND THE WIND, IF THEY DO NOT ENTER INTO OUR DAILY LIVES?"

~ E. M. Forster ~

Special Moment - Week No.52

STAR GAZER

This is such a therapeutic activity.

Simply go out and look at the stars together.

Take in the stunning wonders, connect with your teen and then find your places in the universe.

Be at peace in one another's company.

Anika Vassell is the founder of Starburst Educational Support Services, and developer of the Parent & Teen Relationship Toolkits. The toolkits are the first step-by-step programmes of support for parents who want to better understand, connect, guide & protect their children from modern day teen risks and support them to future success.

With an MSc in Forensic Psychology, Anika has spent more than twenty years working with teenagers all over the UK. A move into secondary school teaching within the leafy suburbs led her to realise that teens from all backgrounds were very much disconnected from their parents.

Now with her own consultancy business, Anika works to share her knowledge with parents worldwide, who have children of adolescent age and gives practical solutions to the often 'testing' years.

Further Parent & Teen Relationship Toolkits that are available:

Create a Circle of Happiness Around Your Teen

Parent Your Teen to High Self Esteem

How to Talk to Your Teen about Drugs, Alcohol & Tobacco

Improve Your Parent & Teen Relationship in Just Six Weeks

http://www.starburst-ess.co.uk/support-your-teen-to-success/

For more information about Anika and how she can further support you and your teen visit:

www.starburst-ess.com
info@starburst-ess.co.uk

14194160R00065

Printed in Great Britain
by Amazon.co.uk, Ltd.,
Marston Gate.